CHAIN REACTI☢NS

From Newton's Rainbow to Frozen Light

Discovering Light

John Farndon

Heinemann LIBRARY

www.heinemann.co.uk/library

Visit our website to find out more information about Heinemann Library books.

To order:

☎ Phone 44 (0) 1865 888066
🖹 Send a fax to 44 (0) 1865 314091
💻 Visit the Heinemann Bookshop at www.heinemann.co.uk/library to browse our catalogue and order online.

Produced for Heinemann Library by White-Thomson Publishing Ltd, Bridgewater Business Centre, 210 High Street, Lewes, East Sussex BN7 2NH

First published in Great Britain by Heinemann Library, Jordan Hill, Oxford OX2 8EJ, part of Harcourt Education.

Heinemann Library is a registered trademark of Harcourt Education Ltd.

Consultant: Ann Fullick, Webucators
Commissioning editors: Andrew Farrow and
    Steve White-Thomson
Editors: Ruth Nason, Richard Woodham
Proofreader: Catherine Clarke
Design: Tim Mayer
Picture research: Amy Sparks
Artwork: William Donohoe

Originated by RMW
Printed and bound in China by Leo Paper Group Ltd

10 digit ISBN 0431186588
13 digit ISBN 978-0-431-18658-0
11 10 09 08 07
10 9 8 7 6 5 4 3 2 1

British Library Cataloguing in Publication Data
Farndon, John
From Newton's Rainbow to Frozen Light:
Discovering Light
535

A full catalogue record for this book is available from the British Library.

Acknowledgements
The author and publisher would like to thank the following for allowing their pictures to be reproduced in this publication: Corbis pp. 4b (Stephanie Maze), 7, 10 (Matthias Kulka/zefa), 13 (Jim Craigmyle), 22 (Ken Redding), 33 (Bettmann), 36 (DK Limited), 45 (Alexander Natruskin/ Reuters), 50 (Rick Friedman), 53 (C. Lackner), 55 (Amit Dave/Reuters), and cover (Lawrence Manning); DigitalVision p. 54; Getty/Taxi p. 46 (Lester Lefkowitz); i-Stockphoto.com pp. 4t, 6 (Tina Rencelj), 15 (David MacFarlane), 17 (Jenn Borton), 27 (Nicholas Belton), 34 (Marcin Pawlik), 39; NASA p. 29; Michael Nason p. 8; Paramount Television/The Kobal Collection p. 32; Science Photo Library pp. 12 (Tony McConnell), 18 (John Chumack), 21 (Ralph Eagle), 23 (Mark A. Schneider), 25 (Sheila Terry), 28t (Andrew Lambert Photography), 28b (Department of Physics, Imperial College), 35 (Robert Gendler), 40 (Andrew Lambert Photography), 41 (American Institute of Physics), 47 (Alfred Pasieka), 49 (European Southern Observatory), 51 (Sam Ogden); Topfoto.co.uk pp. 14 (Topham Picturepoint), 31 (Roger-Viollet/Topfoto), 37 (Topfoto/The Image Works), 43 (Topham/Chapman).

Cover design by Tim Mayer.

Every effort has been made to contact copyright holders of any material reproduced in this book. Any omissions will be rectified in subsequent printings if notice is given to the publishers.

Contents

Any words appearing in the text in bold, **like this**, are explained in the Glossary.

Amazing light

Light is the fastest thing in the Universe. It can travel seven times around the world in less than a second! But did you know that scientists have learned to make light move more slowly than a bicycle? They can also make a particle of light jump across a room in no time at all, and do many other amazing things with light.

What is light?

The light we see is just one of various streams of energy that shoot through the Universe all the time. These streams are called **electromagnetic radiation** and include radio waves, microwaves, and X-rays, as well as light rays. Scientists sometimes call all these types of radiation "light". Visible light is the only type we can see with our eyes, and until barely 130 years ago it was the only type known.

Few things are more important to life than light. We need light to see. Light from the Sun is the source of nearly all energy and warmth. Plants grow by taking in light.

The first known experiments with light were carried out by Mo-Tzu (470–391 BC) and his followers in China. Mo-Tzu knew that light travels in straight lines or rays. He observed that light shining into a house through a pinhole in the blinds could project a vague picture of the world outside into the room. He realized that this happens because the pinhole lets through only a single ray from each point of the scene outside.

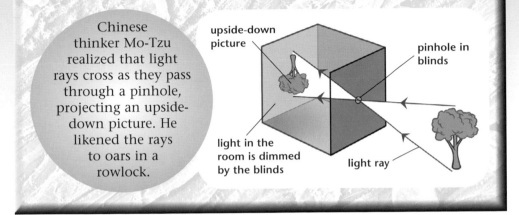

Chinese thinker Mo-Tzu realized that light rays cross as they pass through a pinhole, projecting an upside-down picture. He likened the rays to oars in a rowlock.

upside-down picture

pinhole in blinds

light in the room is dimmed by the blinds

light ray

The search to discover what light is began thousands of years ago. Ancient Greek and Arab scholars made important early contributions, but our understanding of light really began to emerge in the 17th century, with the great English scientist Sir Isaac Newton (1643–1727).

Newton, though, set going a controversy which has raged fiercely ever since. He suggested that light travels as particles. Other scientists argued that light travels as waves.

The waves or particles controversy

No controversy in science has ever lasted as long as this one. Also, no other controversy has revealed so much, not just about light but about the whole Universe – matter, space, and time. Even recent discoveries have not resolved the question, but have opened up new lines of battle. Scientists debate energetically over fantastic ideas such as travelling back in time and leaping instantly across the Universe. All the arguments and discoveries have led to some remarkable modern technologies, including the **laser** and fast-as-light telecommunications.

Rays of light

Scholars knew long ago that light travels in straight lines, often called rays. This explains why you cannot see round corners. But it took the genius of an Arab scholar called Alhazen (AD c.965–1038) to work out how light enables us to see things.

Ancient Greek scholars thought a lot about how we see. Empedocles (c.490–c.430 BC) thought that we see things because our eyes send out light rays which bounce off things and come back to our eyes. Other Greek thinkers believed that we see things because unimaginably thin layers peel off them and travel to our eyes.

Alhazen realized that most light comes from hot light sources such as candles and the Sun.

It was Ibn al-Haitham, better known as Alhazen, who worked out what really happens. He was born in Basra, in what is now southern Iraq, and was one of many brilliant Arab scholars in the early Islamic empire. The story goes that the king of Egypt asked Alhazen to devise a scheme to control the floods of the Nile. Alhazen failed and, to avoid the king's anger, pretended to be mad. While hiding in his room, he began to study light and wrote a book about it called *The Book of Optics*. Optics is the science of light.

Where does light come from?

Alhazen made many clever observations and carried out many experiments. He worked out that light rays come from hot light sources, such as the Sun and candles. He realized that, as the rays travel, they bounce off objects in their path in all directions. We see the rays that bounce off objects towards our eyes.

Did Alhazen invent the camera?

Like Mo-Tzu in China (see page 5), Alhazen observed that light coming through a pinhole in a window blind could create a picture in the room. He realized that the picture would be clearer if the room was completely dark, except for the light from the pinhole. A dark room like this later became known as a **camera obscura** (Latin for "dark room").

The camera obscura became fashionable in the 18th century. This drawing shows how a picture is formed on a screen in the dark room.

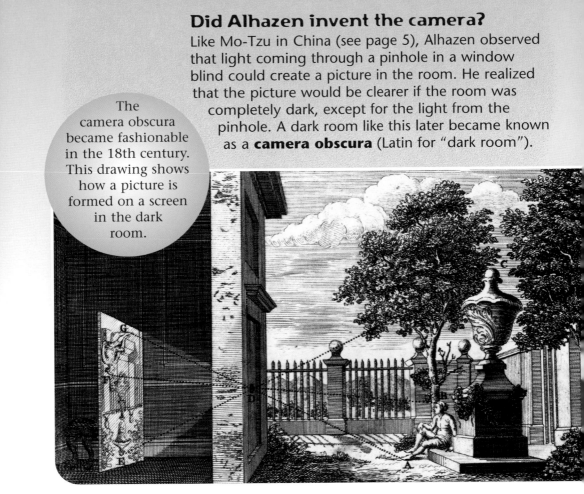

A modern camera is basically a small camera obscura. In a camera, a lens in the hole makes the picture, called the **image**, clearer. Film or photocells are used to record the image.

Alhazen suggested that light rays shine through our eyes and create little images of the world inside them. In fact, our eyes are rather like cameras, taking pictures of the world.

THAT'S AMAZING!

Light rays travel into our eyes in the same way as they enter a camera obscura. The rays cross and therefore project a picture that is upside down. Our clever brain knows this and adjusts, so that we see the picture in our mind the right way up.

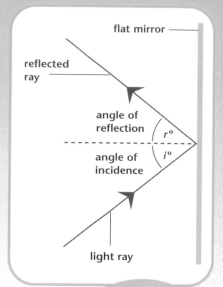

flat mirror

reflected ray

angle of reflection

$r°$

$i°$

angle of incidence

light ray

Bending light

Ancient Greek scholars realized that if light rays are straight lines, you can use **geometry** to study them – and that's what the Greek mathematician Euclid (325–265 BC) did. He investigated the way light rays are **reflected** off shiny surfaces such as mirrors. He showed that rays are reflected off a flat mirror at the same angle as they strike it.

The Greek scholar Diocles (240–180 BC) studied how light reflects off dishes called burning mirrors. People used these dishes to concentrate the Sun's rays and start fires. Diocles realized that as the Sun's rays are reflected off different parts of the curved inside of the dish, they are all directed towards the same point or "focus", creating a hot spot.

When light rays are reflected, the angle of reflection (r) is always the same as the angle at which the ray strikes the mirror, known as the angle of incidence (i).

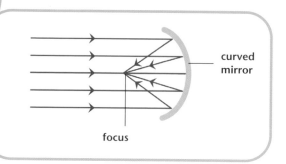

curved mirror

focus

A few centuries later, the Roman scholar Ptolemy (AD 85–165) realized that when light rays enter a substance such as water or glass, they are **refracted** – that is, they bend. Ptolemy wondered whether rays bend more if they enter the substance at a steeper angle. He wasn't quite right, but his idea pointed later researchers in the correct direction.

Light rays travelling to our eyes from the spoon are refracted as they pass from water through glass and into air. This makes the spoon look broken.

The lens

Ibn Sahl (940–c.1000) was an Arab from the same time as Alhazen. Building on Ptolemy's ideas, he tried to work out what happened to light refracted through a domed disc of glass. Ibn Sahl realized that the steeper the curve of the glass, the more the light rays are refracted. Domed glass can bring light rays to a focus, just like Diocles' curved mirror.

Ibn Sahl was thinking of starting fires better, but he had made a momentous discovery: the lens. A few centuries later, glassmakers began to grind and polish glass to make lenses for spectacles. In the 16th century, lenses were combined to make telescopes and then microscopes. Now lenses have a huge range of uses, from cameras to **optical** barcode readers.

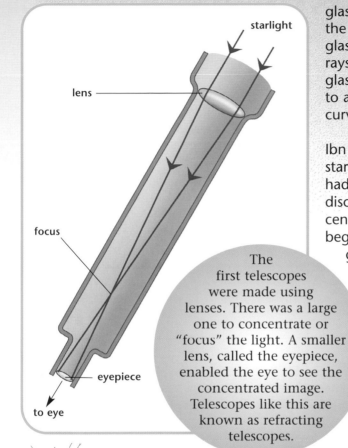

starlight

lens

focus

eyepiece

to eye

The first telescopes were made using lenses. There was a large one to concentrate or "focus" the light. A smaller lens, called the eyepiece, enabled the eye to see the concentrated image. Telescopes like this are known as refracting telescopes.

WHO INVENTED THE TELESCOPE?

The great Italian scientist Galileo (1564–1642) is sometimes said to have invented the telescope. He was certainly the first to look at the Moon and stars through one, in 1609, and his was the first high-quality telescope. But he actually got the idea from cheap novelty telescopes called perspecilliums. These had been invented a few years earlier by Dutch glassmakers, such as Hans Lippershey (c.1570–1619) and Zaccharias Janssen (c.1588–c.1631). And even 340 years before that, an English monk, Roger Bacon (1220–1292), had proposed putting two lenses together, to see the Moon closer.

Colours of light

When Galileo created the first proper telescope in 1609, he was inspired by a novelty sold at a fair. Another novelty from a fair led Isaac Newton to groundbreaking insights into the nature of light and colour.

In 1664, while a student at Cambridge University, Newton went to Stourbridge Fair and bought a novelty called a **prism**. This was a long triangular wedge of glass. Newton took it home and began to experiment in a darkened room, with just a slit in the blinds to let in sunlight.

To his excitement, Newton saw a rainbow strip of colours where sunlight shone through the prism. This strip of colours is called a **spectrum**. People had seen colours like this before but, with a leap of imagination, Newton worked out how they formed. At that time, people thought that colours were various mixes of darkness and lightness. Newton realized that sunlight, which is pretty much white, contains all colours ready-made. The prism splits sunlight into the colours.

When a beam of white light shines through a prism, it splits into different colours. Newton realized that white light contains all these colours.

"If I have seen further, it is by standing on the shoulders of giants."
Newton wrote this in a letter to the English scientist Robert Hooke
(1635–1703), who was his rival. It is said to be a sign of Newton's modesty.
In fact, Newton was probably making fun of Hooke, who was very short.

Colour and light

In case the colours came from the prism, Newton
put a second prism in the path of the light to see
if it added colours. It didn't. It was clear that the
colours came from sunlight alone. Without light,
Newton realized, there is no colour. What is more,
he showed that he could recombine the spectrum
into white light by turning the second prism up the
other way. He had proved that all colours of light
are a part of white light.

Newton went on to suggest why a prism creates
a spectrum. Light is **refracted**
by the glass. Each colour in
the light is refracted at a
different angle and so
separates out.

Newton
realized that a
telescope could be
made using a curved
mirror to focus the light.
Telescopes like this are
known as reflecting
telescopes.

HOW DID NEWTON CHANGE THE TELESCOPE?

In Newton's day astronomers'
telescopes often suffered from
coloured blurring, now called
chromatic aberration. Newton
realized that this happened because
light splits into colours as it is
refracted through the edge of a
lens. To cure the problem, he
devised a new type of telescope
using curved mirrors, instead of
lenses, to focus the light rays. Today
most big telescopes for astronomy
are reflecting telescopes like this.

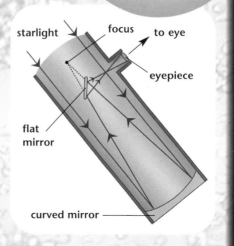

starlight · focus · to eye · eyepiece · flat mirror · curved mirror

Invisible light

Newton showed that white light contains all the colours of the rainbow. What he didn't know was that it contains other colours as well, colours that we cannot see.

It was obvious that sunlight gives warmth and so, in 1800, the British astronomer William Herschel (1738–1822) began to experiment with a prism to see which colour of light produces the most warmth. His idea was simple. He moved a slit along the prism to reveal each of the colours in turn, and measured the temperature of each colour with a thermometer. He found that the blue end of the spectrum is cooler and the red end is warmer.

To make sure that he had included all the red, Herschel moved his thermometer into the shadow beyond. To his astonishment, the temperature rose further. He had discovered an invisible colour of light beyond red, which gives out a lot of heat. Herschel called it infrared.

Thermograms, such as this one showing the body heat of a cyclist, work by detecting infrared light – heat radiation. Different colours show different temperatures, from hot (white) to cold (blue).

Colour beyond violet

A few years after the discovery of infrared, German scientist Johann Ritter (1776–1810) decided to look for invisible light at the other end of the spectrum. He guessed that this end, beyond violet, would be too cool to detect with a thermometer. Instead, he wondered if he could detect invisible light using silver nitrate crystals, which turn black when exposed to light.

Ritter's hunch paid off. When he put paper soaked in silver nitrate in the shadow beyond violet, the paper turned dark. This showed that it was being hit by invisible light. This light came to be called ultraviolet or UV.

Ultraviolet light is sometimes called "black" light because our eyes cannot see it. It can be useful in detective work because it reveals otherwise invisible signs such as hidden fingerprints.

HOW WAS PHOTOGRAPHY INVENTED?

The way that light turns silver nitrate black enabled Johann Ritter to discover ultraviolet light. Frenchman Joseph Niépce (1765–1833) wondered if silver nitrate could be used to capture the picture projected inside a **camera obscura**. A metal plate coated in grains of silver nitrate could be put inside the camera and would turn dark wherever bright light fell on it. The idea worked – but the picture quickly turned black once exposed to daylight. Next Niépce tried coating the plate with a bitumen-like substance, which went grey when struck by light. With this he made the world's first ever photograph in 1826, but it was very blurred. Helped by Jacques Louis Daguerre (1787–1851), Niépce looked for a way to "fix" silver nitrate so that a picture would not turn black. In 1837 Daguerre succeeded and so created the first successful photographic process.

How light moves

Newton's discovery that white light contains all the colours of the rainbow was a great breakthrough. Next he thought about what light is and how it moves. He explained his theories in a book called *Opticks* (1704).

Newton's big idea was that a beam of light is made of countless tiny particles travelling at enormous speed. Rays of light, Newton believed, are the tracks of these fast-moving particles, which he called **corpuscles**. If light is bullet-like corpuscles, he argued, this would explain why light travels in straight lines and casts shadows. Like bullets, light cannot bend around objects in its path.

The corpuscle idea would also explain why a mirror **reflects** light: the corpuscles bounce off the mirror, like tennis balls bouncing off a wall. Even **refraction** might be explained by the corpuscles accelerating as they pass from air into glass or water. Most significantly, the corpuscle theory would explain how light can travel through empty space, which it clearly does since you can see stars.

Isaac Newton did not only transform ideas about light. He also devised theories of motion to explain all movement in the Universe, and he introduced the idea of gravity. This bust shows Newton in 1718.

Newton's waves?

It is sometimes said that Newton believed only that light is particles, while others argued that light is waves. This is not strictly true. Newton argued that a ray of light is a fast-moving particle, but he also suggested that, when a ray is refracted or reflected, it creates colours by vibrating – that is, by making waves. This is how he explained why things are coloured even though we cannot see colours in a beam of sunlight. Colour, he said, is simply the sensation produced by the vibrations or waves "beating and dashing against [...] the eye", like sound waves on the ear, or real waves on the seashore.

Newton believed, moreover, that the size of the vibrations determines the colour. Here he was right, as we shall see. However, Newton never explained the wave part of his theory very clearly, and it was later forgotten.

Shimmering, multi-coloured bands like these on oil are found in many places. Newton observed them between two sheets of glass pressed together, which is why they are called "Newton's rings". We now know they are caused by **interference** (see page 21).

THAT'S AMAZING!

Newton went to extraordinary lengths to study light and vision. Once he tried repeatedly staring at the Sun's reflection in a mirror, in order to see the **after-image** when he turned his eyes to a dark corner. This was a very dangerous thing to do. Luckily for him, he was only blinded for a few days. Then he tried ramming a knife between his eyeball and the socket, to see how squeezing the eyeball affected his sight. Again he was lucky to escape unharmed.

Huygens's waves

Newton's influence was very powerful, but not everyone agreed with him. Dutch scientist Christiaan Huygens (1629–1693) argued that light travels not as particles but as waves, like ripples on a pond.

If light travels as waves, Huygens showed, then it is easy to explain why light is refracted. Imagine a line of soldiers marching in perfect step. If the line hits a muddy patch at an angle, the soldiers at one end step into the mud and are slowed down. The others carry on at the old speed until they too hit the mud. The effect is to make the line veer round.

It is the same with a wave of light hitting glass. If light travels more slowly through glass than through air, then, as it moves from one substance to the other, it is skewed round or refracted.

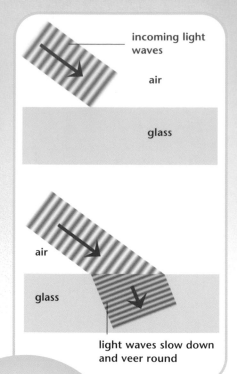

incoming light waves

air

glass

air

glass

light waves slow down and veer round

Light bends as it passes from air into glass. To explain why this happens, Dutch scientist Christiaan Huygens likened a light wave to a line of soldiers marching from dry ground into muddy ground.

? HOW DID HUYGENS'S WAVES WORK?

In 1679 Huygens explained how light becomes a wave. Imagine a stone thrown into a pond. Ripples spread out around it. If a handful of stones are thrown in, some ripples from each run against each other and are cancelled out, but all the ripples moving in roughly the same direction combine into one general "wave front". It is the same, Huygens said, with light rippling out from different points on, for example, a candle flame.

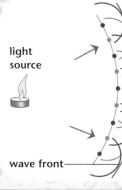

light source

wave front

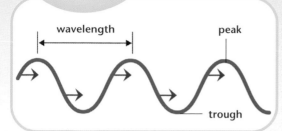

Explaining the spectrum

Huygens went on to explain the **spectrum** in the following way. Each colour of light has a different **wavelength**. When light travels from one substance to the other, the degree of refraction – that is, the amount the light is skewed round – depends on the wavelength of light. The shorter the wavelength, the more it is bent. Light waves at the red end of the spectrum have greater wavelengths than light waves at the blue end, and so red light is bent less than blue.

Two theories in conflict

Scientists were presented with a dilemma. Newton's corpuscle theory explained very well why you cannot see around corners and why things cast sharp shadows, but it did not give a good explanation for refraction or the spectrum. Huygens's wave theory, on the other hand, explained refraction and the spectrum well, but it did not explain why light casts sharp shadows and cannot go around corners. Nor did the wave theory explain how light travels through empty space, in which there is nothing to wave.

The speed of light

The ancient Greek thinker Aristotle thought that light reaches us in no time at all – no matter how far it travels. In the 17th century he was finally proved wrong.

Alhazen in the 10th century and Roger Bacon in the 13th were both sure that light, like sound, does take time to travel – but they had no way to show it. Therefore, in the 17th century, most scientists still believed that light moves instantaneously, as Aristotle said. Galileo tried to measure the speed of light using lanterns on distant hills, but light travels much too fast to be measured over such a short distance.

Then, in 1675, a young Danish astronomer called Ole Römer (1644–1710) was studying the moons of the planet Jupiter. Strangely, they did not seem to circle Jupiter at an even speed. They appeared to slow down and speed up again every 400 days. Römer knew that Jupiter comes closest to Earth every 400 days, and wondered if the timings were linked.

Danish astronomer Ole Römer found the first evidence that light takes time to travel when he studied the four then-known moons of Jupiter. These four moons had been discovered by Galileo in 1609, using his new telescope.

Late moons

Römer studied Jupiter's moons for a few years. He found that they seemed to slow down towards the time when Jupiter was furthest from Earth – and seemed to speed up as Jupiter moved closer.

Europa

Ganymede

Io

Callisto

Römer realized the simple reason. The further away that Jupiter was, the longer it took for light from its moons to reach him. This made the moons appear late in their orbit.

Using Römer's figures, Huygens then compared the change in the timing with the change in the distance to Jupiter in order to calculate the speed of light. His answer was 220,000 kilometres (136,700 miles) per second. We now know that the speed of light is nearer 300,000 kilometres (186,000 miles) per second, but that first calculation was a huge step forward.

HOW COULD LIGHT SPEED BE MEASURED?

In 1850 – 175 years after Huygens's calculation – Frenchman Jean Foucault (1819–1868) finally worked out an ingenious way to measure light speed on Earth. He bounced a light beam off a mirror made to spin at high speed. A flat mirror **reflected** the beam back on to the spinning mirror. By this time the spinning mirror had moved round a little way, and so it reflected the light to a slightly different place. By measuring the shift and comparing it to the speed of the mirror's spin, Foucault worked out the speed of light. His figure was 298,000 kilometres (185,180 miles) per second.

This diagram shows a modern version of Foucault's method for measuring the speed of light. Foucault's apparatus included an array of mirrors and a microscope.

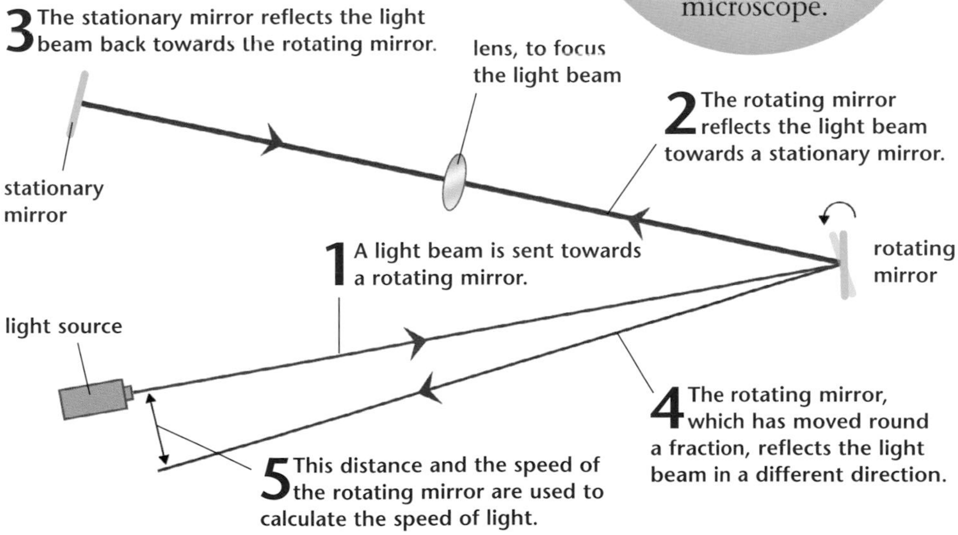

3 The stationary mirror reflects the light beam back towards the rotating mirror.

lens, to focus the light beam

2 The rotating mirror reflects the light beam towards a stationary mirror.

stationary mirror

1 A light beam is sent towards a rotating mirror.

rotating mirror

light source

4 The rotating mirror, which has moved round a fraction, reflects the light beam in a different direction.

5 This distance and the speed of the rotating mirror are used to calculate the speed of light.

The wave theory proved?

So great was Newton's influence that for a century or more his theory that light is particles held sway. Then, in 1801, a brilliant amateur scientist named Thomas Young (1773–1829) performed a now famous experiment.

Young was willing to try his hand at anything. He was called the "Young Phenomenon" for reading 5 languages fluently by the age of 13. As an adult he made the first modern translation of Egyptian hieroglyphics and also devised a measure of elasticity in substances, which is still used today. Yet he is most famous for his double-slit experiment.

The idea began when Young was looking at the patterns of light made by a candle shining through a mist of fine water droplets. He saw coloured rings around a bright centre and wondered if they might be caused by waves of light interacting. Maybe Newton was wrong after all.

The double-slit experiment

Young showed how when light shines through two slits, it spreads out and interacts (interferes), giving bright and dark bands on a screen, such as some paper.

To test his idea, Young devised a simple but ingenious experiment. He shone a beam of light on to two slits in a piece of card. Light shining through the slits created an intriguing pattern on some paper beyond them.

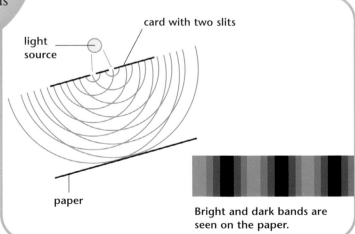

light source

card with two slits

paper

Bright and dark bands are seen on the paper.

If light was streams of particles, you should simply get two pools of light directly beyond each slit. Instead, Young saw bright and dark bands, like a fuzzy barcode.

Young argued that, as light waves spread out beyond the slits, they interact. If two waves ripple up at the same time, they make a wave twice as big – creating the bright bands. If one wave ripples up as another is rippling down, they cancel each other out – creating the dark bands. This is called **interference**.

Young went on to show that different colours of light create different interference patterns. This demonstrated that the colour of light depends on its **wavelength**.

Young realized that the results of his experiment could be explained by light waves interfering in two ways. Constructive interference gives the bright bands of the pattern. Destructive interference gives the dark bands.

Constructive interference: two waves whose peaks coincide add to each other's strength.

Destructive interference: two waves cancel each other out, as the peaks of one coincide with the troughs of the other.

THAT'S AMAZING!

When Newton studied the **spectrum**, he identified seven colours: red, orange, yellow, green, blue, indigo, and violet. In fact, the spectrum is a continuous gradation of colours. Yet, in the 19th century, scientists such as Thomas Young and James Clerk Maxwell (1831–1879) realized that all the colours can be made by adding together three "primary" coloured lights in different proportions. We now know that these **primary colours** of light are red, green, and blue.

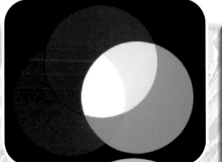

Red, green, and blue are the primary colours of light, from which all other colours can be made.

21

Light around corners

Independently of Young, a French army engineer called Augustin Fresnel (1788–1827) was also coming up with evidence to demolish the theory that light is particles. Fresnel was studying a phenomenon called **diffraction**.

Diffraction had been identified in 1665 by Francesco Grimaldi, an Italian priest. He noticed that objects don't block off light as completely as you might think. A little light always creeps around the edge of objects in its path. You can see this in the "halo" around a person's head when you look at them against the sunset. The result is that shadows are very slightly smaller and fuzzier than they should be if light were bullet-like particles. If you look closely at a shadow, you can see little bands of light and dark around the edge. This spillage of light into shadow is caused by diffraction.

The slight "halo" seen around this person shows that she is not completely blocking the light that strikes her far side.

Diffraction waves

Newton thought that diffraction occurs because light rays are deflected slightly as they pass close to an object. Fresnel was convinced that a better explanation came from considering light as waves.

Every now and then, typically when the air is cold or damp, you can see a halo around the Moon. The halo is called a corona, and is caused by the diffraction of moonlight through countless tiny drops of water or ice crystals in the air. Coronas also form around the Sun, but you should never look directly at the Sun.

In 1817 Fresnel began a series of incredibly precise experiments – and detected tiny interference bands like those behind Young's double slit. Fresnel backed up his experiments with detailed calculations based on Huygens's idea of a moving wave front, to show how waves produce diffraction.

Like Young, however, Fresnel met with fierce opposition, not least from a brilliant mathematician called Siméon-Denis Poisson (1781–1840). Poisson used Fresnel's calculations to show that there should be a small bright spot behind an object in the path of a light beam. This, Poisson said, was clearly absurd and so it showed how silly Fresnel's idea was. Then another scientist, Dominique Arago (1786–1853), conducted an experiment – and found the bright spot just where predicted! Fresnel was right.

Diffraction can create a bright spot behind a solid object in the path of a light beam.

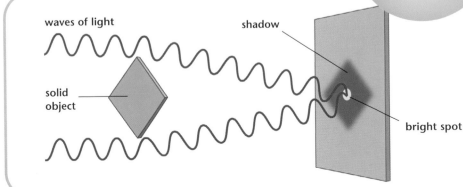

waves of light

shadow

solid object

bright spot

Waves in the ether

Young's and Fresnel's experiments seemed to show that light is a wave, and not a particle. But what is waving and what are the waves like?

Victorian scientists knew that if light is a wave, it must wave something. They began to talk about "ether", a word used by the ancient Greek thinker Aristotle for a mysterious substance that, he believed, must fill the space between the stars. Victorian scientists sometimes distinguished their idea as "luminiferous [light-bearing] aether", but it was no less vague than Aristotle's. For them, ether was an invisible, undetectable substance which was spread through everything – empty space, air, water, and glass – and which transmitted light.

Since Young and Fresnel had shown light to be a wave, most scientists became convinced that ether was real. Then Young and Fresnel had further ideas about how light waves move, which made it even harder to imagine what ether could be.

HOW DID FRESNEL DISCOVER POLARIZED LIGHT?

In 1808, in Paris, French colonel Etienne Malus (1775–1812) was looking through a crystal of **Iceland spar** at the **reflections** in some windows. He noticed that the crystal became brighter or darker as he turned it. Hearing about this, Fresnel worked out that most light vibrates at pretty much every angle but, when light is reflected, the vibrations in all but one plane are cancelled out. The light is said to be polarized. Fresnel suggested that the polarized light reflected from the windows would only shine through the crystal when the crystal was held so that microscopic slots in it lined up with the plane of the polarized light.

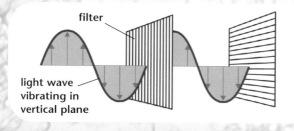

filter

light wave vibrating in vertical plane

Polarized light vibrates in only one plane, and so it passes through a filter only if the filter's "slots" are at the necessary angle.

Things that don't show when seen in normal light may be revealed by polarized light. Here polarized light has been used to show up defects and stresses in the plastic lenses of some glasses.

Transverse waves

Most scientists thought that light waves roll forward like sound waves, squeezing and releasing the ether on their way – like a push along a "slinky" spring. In that case, ether could be a substance like a fluid or air. However, this was put in doubt by Fresnel's discovery of polarization.

Polarized light vibrates in only one plane. Young and Fresnel realized that it could only be explained by light waves moving up and down or side to side, as when a skipping rope is shaken. These are called transverse waves.

A longitudinal wave starts with to-and-fro movement.

A transverse wave starts with up-and-down, or side-to-side, movement.

To transmit transverse waves, ether would need to be solid enough to waggle – at least as solid as jelly. How could such a substance be spread through everything and yet impossible to detect? It made no sense. Yet most scientists believed that it would be understood eventually.

A "slinky" spring shows how longitudinal waves, such as sound waves, move. A skipping rope shows transverse waves. Young and Fresnel said that light waves are like this.

TALKING SCIENCE

In the 1770s, the dictionary writer Samuel Johnson summed up the difficulty of describing light: *"We all <u>know</u> what light is; but it is not easy to <u>tell</u> what it is."*

The electromagnetic spectrum

On 12 March 1832, the British scientist Michael Faraday (1791–1867) wrote, "I am inclined to think the vibratory theory [of electromagnetism] will apply [...] most probably to light". He sealed the words in an envelope, to be opened when he died. By a leap of imagination Faraday had guessed not only that electricity and magnetism spread as waves, but also that they are related to light.

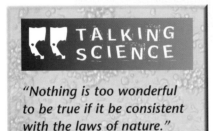

The link between electricity and magnetism had only recently been discovered. Various scientists had found that electricity is magnetic and that magnetism can create electricity. It was Faraday who showed that electricity and magnetism are simply two different faces of the same force – electromagnetism. Faraday also had the idea that this force makes itself felt in an area or "field" around each magnet or electric current.

The range of colours of light is just part of a broad span of electromagnetic waves. This span ranges from radio waves to gamma rays and is known as the electromagnetic spectrum.

Electromagnetic waves

Faraday decided, after all, to reveal his ideas before he died. In 1846, in a lecture at London's Royal Institution, he explained that electromagnetic force is transmitted by vibrations or waves, which have no need of ether. He said that light is a such a wave.

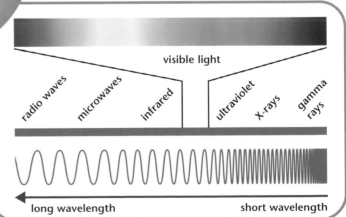

visible light

radio waves   microwaves   infrared   ultraviolet   X-rays   gamma rays

long wavelength ← → short wavelength

So far this was only speculation. Then a brilliant young Scottish scientist, James Clerk Maxwell (1831–1879), began to analyse electromagnetic waves. He came up with four equations showing how an electromagnetic field is created by waves. He also worked out by ingenious maths that, at a particular speed, an electric wave and a magnetic wave can help each other to whizz along. This speed was 300,000 kilometres (186,000 miles) per second, the same as the speed of light. Maxwell knew this could not be coincidence. Light must be a type of electromagnetic wave.

WHAT TYPES OF ELECTROMAGNETIC WAVES WERE DISCOVERED?

Light and heat (infrared light) were the only types of electromagnetic waves known to Faraday and Maxwell, although Maxwell reasoned that there must be other invisible types with different wavelengths. Over the next half-century, other scientists discovered them. In 1888, German physicist Heinrich Hertz (1857–1894) discovered radio waves. In 1895, Wilhelm Röntgen (1845–1893), another German, discovered X-rays. We now know that light is simply the visible part of a continuous range or spectrum of electromagnetic waves of different lengths, from long-wave radio waves to short-wave **gamma rays**.

X-rays have a shorter wavelength than light. When directed at a body, some are absorbed while others pass through, to make a picture on a photographic plate.

Chemical light

In the 18th century scientists had realized that many substances burn with distinctive coloured flames. By shining a flame through a **prism** to create a **spectrum**, they could study its spread of colours precisely. This is called spectroscopy. Light from the Sun and stars can be studied in the same way.

Two pioneers of spectroscopy were Robert Bunsen (1811–1899) and Gustav Kirchhoff (1824–1887). They tested the flames of thousands of substances. Kirchhoff found that when any **chemical element** burns, it gives a unique spectrum, which identifies it like a fingerprint. The spectrum is not continuous, like a rainbow. Instead, it has bright lines of certain colours, with dark bands in between. Bright-line spectra like these are sometimes called "emission" spectra, because they show the colours emitted when an element burns.

Kirchhoff then found another type of spectrum, now called an absorption spectrum. It is created by shining light through a gas. Elements in the gas absorb certain colours in the light, producing dark lines in the spectrum. The dark lines of an absorption spectrum appear in exactly the same positions as the bright lines of the emission spectrum of the same substance.

German scientist Robert Bunsen is famous for the gas burner he devised for testing the flames of different substances. Here, copper is being tested.

This photograph shows the bright-line spectrum for helium gas. The colour lines are the colours emitted by glowing helium.

Kirchhoff's discoveries meant that scientists could tell what the Sun and even the most distant stars are made of, by analysing the spectra of their light. Kirchhoff analysed light from the Sun and found that it contains gold, among other substances. Norman Lockyer (1836–1920) and Pierre Janssen (1824–1907) even discovered a new element by analysing the Sun's light. This was **helium**, named after the Greek Sun-god Helios. It was another 25 years before helium was found on Earth.

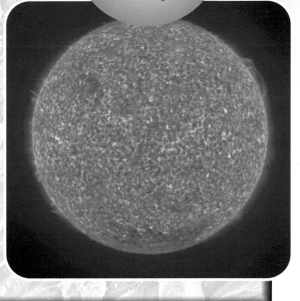

This photograph of the Sun was taken using an Extreme Ultraviolet Imaging Telescope.

Colour and atoms

In 1885 a Swiss schoolteacher, Johann Balmer (1828–1898), analysed mathematically the spread of **wavelengths** emitted by hydrogen gas. He chose hydrogen because its spectrum was thought to have just four lines. Balmer found a simple equation linking the wavelengths of the four lines. It became known as the Balmer series.

By this time, scientists knew that elements got their identities from their own special **atom**, and so they reasoned that each element's distinctive spectrum must have something to do with its atom. Scientists guessed that each type of atom must emit a unique pattern of light. If so, James Clerk Maxwell suggested, maybe the atom was not a solid ball, as everyone thought. Perhaps different wavelengths were created by different vibrations inside the atom. It turned out that he was right.

The fastest thing in the Universe

Michael Faraday suggested that light waves travel with no need of any substance like ether, but most other scientists, including James Clerk Maxwell, disagreed. In the second half of the 19th century, the hunt was on to find the ether at last.

A German American called Albert Michelson (1852–1931) and his American colleague, Edward Morley (1838–1923), developed an idea first suggested by Maxwell. It was clear, they said, that as the Earth rotates, it must move through the ether. If they could project a beam of light in the same direction as the Earth moves, the light would be travelling through the ether as if it were swimming upstream. The flow of ether – which they called the ether wind – would slow down the light beam. If Michelson and Morley could detect just a slight slowing in the speed of light in the direction of the Earth's rotation, they would have found the ether.

? HOW COULD LIGHT BEHAVE LIKE A SWIMMER?

To explain why the speed of light should vary if ether exists, Michelson pictured two equally fast swimmers. One swims 25 metres (82 feet) across a fast-flowing river and back. The other swims 25 metres (82 feet) down the river and back.

The swimmer heading across the river has to swim slightly further to compensate for the current sweeping him downstream. The other swimmer is aided by the current at first, but he must fight against it as he heads upstream again.

Simple maths shows that the swimmer going across the river gets back first – so must be quicker. Michelson believed that, in the same way, light would seem to move faster across the ether wind than straight into it.

Trying to catch the wind

Michelson and Morley developed Jean Foucault's idea of measuring the speed of light using a spinning mirror. They also floated their entire equipment on mercury in order to minimize vibrations. This would ensure that their measurements were precise. Yet despite all precautions and years of effort, Michelson and Morley could never detect any difference in speed between light travelling "upstream" through the ether and light travelling across it. Eventually they had to concede that this was not because of a fault in their work. The speed of light is constant in every direction – and so there is no ether.

New light speed

Albert Michelson was one of the first scientists to measure the speed of light really accurately. Here he is shown in his laboratory in 1915.

After his failure to detect ether, Michelson became determined to find the most accurate figure possible for the speed of light. He began to develop the method that Foucault had used in 1850. By 1883 Michelson had measured the speed of light at 299,853 kilometres (185,909 miles) per second.

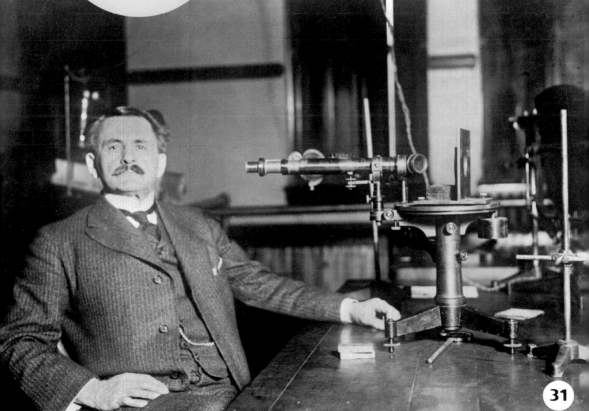

Einstein's Special Relativity

Gradually scientists learned one lesson from the Michelson-Morley experiment – that the ether does not exist. They paid less attention to another – that light always travels at the same speed. One scientist who did think about this was Albert Einstein (1879–1955).

Light is not just the fastest thing in the Universe, Einstein reasoned. It always travels at the same speed, no matter how you measure it. That was shown by Michelson's and Morley's experiment. Moreover, Maxwell's equations gave only one possible speed of light. Light's speed is, as Einstein said, a "constant".

Yet, Einstein realized, every other speed we measure is relative to something else. If you measure how fast you're running, for instance, you measure your speed relative to the ground – which seems still but is, in fact, whirling through space as the Earth moves. The speed of light is the one speed that is not relative.

Einstein's theories show that a spaceship could never travel at the speed of light. Even if it could, it would take years to travel between stars. The starship in the fictional TV series *Star Trek* cheats the light speed limit by using a Warp Drive, which warps space and time around it.

THAT'S AMAZING!

Light takes a certain time to reach us, so we always see things a little while after they happen. The greater the distance, the greater the time delay. The Andromeda galaxy in the night sky is so far away that you see it as it was almost four million years ago!

Albert Einstein's theories of relativity made him the most famous scientist in the world.

Distorting time and distance

Speed is the distance covered in a particular time. If the speed of light does not vary, Einstein realized, time and distance must vary instead. That means that time and distance are relative – and can be distorted. This has little impact on everyday events, but for things moving close to the speed of light, it has some weird effects. Einstein said that, for things travelling at near the speed of light, time would dilate (stretch out) and lengths would shrink.

Einstein's ideas were embodied in his Special Relativity Theory of 1905. This put light at the centre of our understanding of how the Universe works.

WHAT IS GENERAL RELATIVITY?

Einstein imagined a light beam shot across a falling lift. It would hit the opposite side slightly higher up – because the lift falls slightly as the light crosses – and so the light would seem to curve upwards. Reasoning from Special Relativity, Einstein showed that the light is not really curving. It just seems so, because space and time are distorted by the gravity that pulls the lift down.

Einstein went on to develop the idea of General Relativity, in which gravity works by pulling space and time out of shape. Although light always travels in straight lines, Einstein said, it sometimes appears to be bent by powerful gravitational fields.

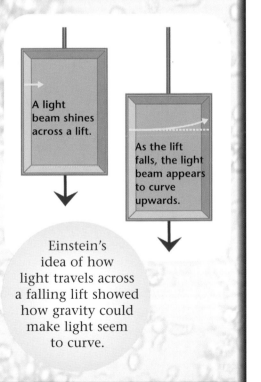

A light beam shines across a lift.

As the lift falls, the light beam appears to curve upwards.

Einstein's idea of how light travels across a falling lift showed how gravity could make light seem to curve.

Particles of light

Given Thomas Young's and Augustin Fresnel's experiments, and James Clerk Maxwell's electromagnetic wave equations, it was not surprising if scientists were certain that light is a wave. Yet the particle idea was not quite dead.

Scientists had long known that light is a form of energy. Gustav Kirchhoff wanted to know if the amount of energy in light depends on its **wavelength**. In the 1880s his experiments with the light of red-hot glowing metal showed that it does.

When metal gets hot, it glows and emits light over the full range of wavelengths. In the 19th century Kirchhoff learned a great deal about light by measuring the amount of energy given off at different wavelengths.

Light at the violet end of the **spectrum** (with the shorter wavelength) is the most energetic. Light at the red end is only half as energetic. Indeed, the relationship between light's energy and its wavelength seemed so marked that scientists began to look for a mathematical equation to sum it up. Lord Rayleigh (1842–1919) soon found an equation that worked with the violet end of the spectrum. Then Wilhelm Wien (1864–1928) found one that worked for the red end. Strangely, no one could find an equation to fit the whole range.

THAT'S AMAZING!

In 1879, Austrian physicist Josef Stefan (1835–1893) worked out that the hotter something gets, the brighter it glows, in a very predictable way. Using this rule (later called the Stefan-Boltzmann Law), Stefan worked out that the surface temperature of the Sun is about 5400 °Celsius (9752 °Fahrenheit). Astronomers have since used the rule to work out how hot many other stars are.

Chunks of light

After years of research, German scientist Max Planck (1858–1947) made a breakthrough, with a single equation for the whole spectrum. Yet this equation worked only if light is emitted in particular bite-size chunks of energy, not in a continuous array as scientists had expected. Planck called these chunks "quanta", from the Latin for "how much". Even he found this hard to accept – for what could chunks of energy be but particles?

Planck's quanta seemed to go completely against a century of mounting evidence for waves. It took the genius of Albert Einstein to bring out the significance of Planck's discovery.

Like red-hot glowing metal, stars radiate light in the full range of wavelengths. But as a star burns hotter, it gets brighter. It also emits more light at the violet end of the spectrum, so that its colour changes from red to blue.

WHAT IS A QUANTUM SCALE?

To see the difference between a continuous scale and a **quantum** scale, think of temperature and money. Temperature rises on a continuous scale. This means that besides, say, 5 and 6 degrees, the temperature can be anything in between, such as 5.7 degrees or 5.83 degrees. A quantum scale is like money. For instance, you can buy something for 5 pence or 6 pence, but not for anything in between.

The discovery of photons

Few people took in the significance of Planck's quanta, except for Einstein. With typical brilliance, he linked quanta to something spotted in 1902 by a Hungarian physicist, Philipp Lenard (1862–1947).

Scientists had known for some time that light can generate electricity. This was later called the **photoelectric effect**. Lenard was exploring it by shining bright lights on to certain metals. He noticed how the impact of light seemed to knock **electrons** off **atoms** in the metals. Electrons are the tiny **subatomic particles** responsible for electricity, and so the effect was to create a little electricity.

One thing surprised Lenard. The maximum energy of electrons knocked out by light of a certain colour was always the same. It didn't matter how bright or dim the light was. The only thing that made a difference was its colour. If light is a wave, you would expect the energy of the electrons to rise with the intensity of the light, regardless of colour. Think how surprised you would be if the amount of sand washed away by waves on the beach was always the same, no matter how big the wave.

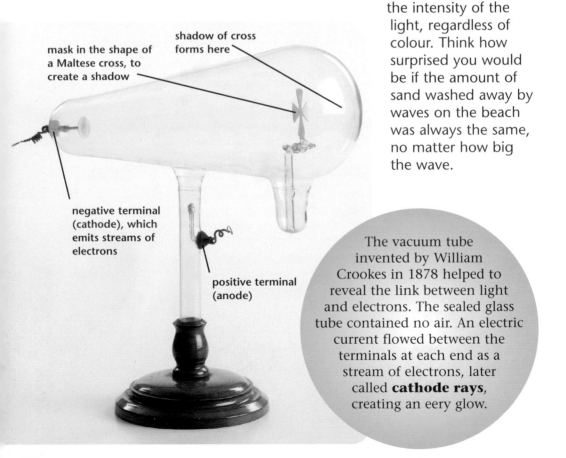

mask in the shape of a Maltese cross, to create a shadow

shadow of cross forms here

negative terminal (cathode), which emits streams of electrons

positive terminal (anode)

The vacuum tube invented by William Crookes in 1878 helped to reveal the link between light and electrons. The sealed glass tube contained no air. An electric current flowed between the terminals at each end as a stream of electrons, later called **cathode rays**, creating an eery glow.

Einstein showed how these apparently weird results could be explained. The trick was to think of light not as waves but as little packets of energy, like Planck's quanta. Electrons would be knocked off atoms only by packets of exactly the right size – not bigger, nor smaller. Planck had thought of quanta just as a mathematical trick. Einstein was saying that they are real, and that light travels in packets of energy. American chemist Gilbert Lewis (1875–1946) eventually gave these packets the name **photons**.

In 1916 another American, Robert Millikan (1868–1953), who was trying to prove Einstein wrong, succeeded only in proving him right. Millikan spent 10 years measuring the photoelectric effect, and all his results turned out exactly as Einstein predicted. In a way, Einstein seemed to be bringing back Newton's ideas about **corpuscles**. However, Einstein's photons are not particles like tiny balls; they can also behave as waves.

? WHO MADE THE FIRST SOLAR CELL?

Solar cells are panels that exploit the photoelectric effect to make electricity from sunlight. The first solar cell was made in 1883, when Charles Fritts coated selenium with a transparently thin layer of gold. Sunlight got electrons moving in the selenium, and the gold conducted the electricity. The cell converted less than 1 per cent of the light falling on it into electricity, but it was a start.

Today whole power plants can be run by solar panels, as here in California, USA.

Light from atoms

By 1910 it was clear to scientists not only that **atoms** both emit and absorb light, but also that all light comes from atoms. Now they had to work out what goes on inside the atom.

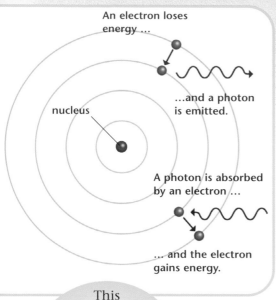

An electron loses energy ...

...and a photon is emitted.

nucleus

A photon is absorbed by an electron ...

... and the electron gains energy.

This diagram shows how photons of light (shown as wavy lines) are absorbed and emitted by electrons (blue dots).

Experiments in the 1890s had shown that atoms are not solid, but contain **electrons** – and that it is electrons that send out and soak up **photons** of light. In 1911 British physicist Ernest Rutherford (1892–1972) found that atoms are largely empty space, with electrons orbiting a tiny, dense **nucleus**. The following year, Danish scientist Niels Bohr (1885–1962) created a remarkable theory to explain why each atom gives a unique array of colours, shown in its line spectrum.

Bohr realized that the pattern of spectral lines corresponds to the atom's arrangement of electrons. Electrons orbiting near the nucleus must have less energy than those far away, Bohr reasoned. What if electrons orbit in a series of rings, each with a particular amount of energy or energy level? The colour and energy of any photon emitted – and so the atom's spectrum – would then depend on how these rings are arranged.

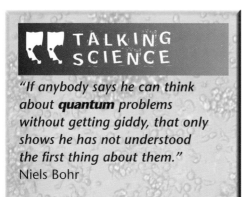

TALKING SCIENCE

*"If anybody says he can think about **quantum** problems without getting giddy, that only shows he has not understood the first thing about them."*
Niels Bohr

How an atom emits light

Imagine Bohr's atom as a circular stadium, with an electron as a ball rolling around the tiers inside. This isn't really what it's like, but it's a good way to think of it. Normally, the electron rolls around the lowest tier or "ground state" near the centre. Every so often the atom gets an energy input – when heated or hit by another particle, for example. It is said to be "excited".

The extra energy lifts the electron to a higher "energy level", a tier further from the centre. How high depends on the size of the energy input. After a while, though, the electron rolls off and drops back – perhaps falling straight to the ground state, or perhaps hitting various tiers on the way down. As it falls, it loses energy, emitting it as a photon of light.

According to Bohr, the energy lost, and so the colour of the photon emitted, depends on the size of drop between tiers. Each atom has a unique pattern of energy levels, and therefore it emits a unique range of colours. As it turned out, Bohr's model only worked well for the simplest atoms such as hydrogen, with just a single electron. Yet it was a major step forward.

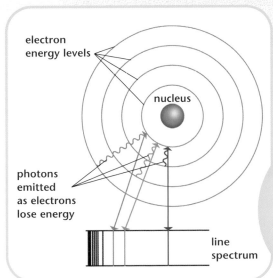

electron energy levels

nucleus

photons emitted as electrons lose energy

line spectrum

The colours of a line spectrum are explained by the release of photons as electrons in the atom drop back to lower energy levels.

HOW DO NEON LIGHTS WORK?

Neon lights, invented in 1915, show Bohr's idea in action.

A neon light is a glass tube filled with neon gas. When switched on, electricity zips along the tube, exciting electrons on the neon atoms and boosting them all to one high energy level. As they drop back, they emit a flood of photons, all the same brilliant red.

Light's split personality

At the start of the 1920s, a few scientists still believed that light must be a wave and that photons, particles of light, were just tricks of mathematics. Then, in 1923, an experiment by Arthur Compton (1892–1962) proved that photons are real. X-rays were fired at graphite, causing light to shoot up in a way that showed that it must be particles. Scientists thus had proof that light is a particle. Yet they already had proof that light is a wave!

A French physics student, Louis de Broglie (1892–1987), suggested that electrons too might be waves as well as particles. He imagined electrons running around an atom's nucleus in wiggly lines. Within a year scientists proved this theory right with a double-slit experiment like the one used by Thomas Young to prove that light is a wave. Electrons fired through the slits produced **interference** bands, just like light waves.

The wave-particle duality

In 1928 Bohr suggested that light and matter can each be both a wave and a particle – but never both at once. This double personality of light and matter is called the "wave-particle duality". Put simply, a photon sets out and arrives as a particle, but travels as a wave.

This pattern is produced when electrons are fired through slits in a sheet of graphite onto a luminescent screen. It is caused by waves of electrons interfering with each other.

With his "uncertainty principle", Werner Heisenberg revolutionized science – showing that there are some things that scientists can never measure with complete certainty.

An ingenious German physicist, Werner Heisenberg (1901–1976), realized a puzzling fact. You can measure the **momentum** and **wavelength** of a photon of light – the moving, wave side of its personality. You can measure its position – where it strikes a target as a particle, for instance. But you can never be sure of both at the same time because, as soon as you try to pin a photon down as a particle, it starts behaving like a wave, and vice versa.

This insight, called the **uncertainty principle**, is not just a problem with measuring. It is a basic property of light and other particles. It means that scientists must think in terms of **probabilities**, not certainties. You can never know with certainty where a photon will go. You can only say where it probably will.

THAT'S AMAZING!

When scientists learned how to do the double-slit experiment with a single photon, they found an amazing proof of Heisenberg's ideas. If the photon is a particle, they expected it to shoot through one slit and hit just a single spot on the target behind. Instead, it seemed to go through both slits at once and interfere with itself on the far side to form interference bands on the target, like waves. And yet, when the scientists tried to observe which slit the photon went to, they found just a single photon – and the interference bands disappeared!

Amazing quanta

The wave-particle duality and the uncertainty principle may have brought scientists closer to the truth about light, but they made life more difficult. Scientists were now working only with probabilities, not certainties. How could they think about what happens to a particular light particle, when its position and its movement are not even certain at one time?

One of the 20th century's greatest physicists, Richard Feynman (1918–1988), devised a way to think about this. He plotted a graph to show the most likely movement of a particle. He and others began to develop a new science of light and matter called **quantum electrodynamics** (QED).

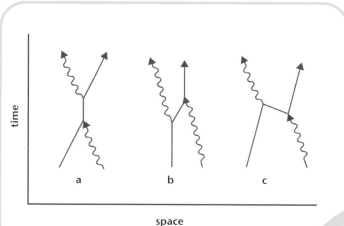

QED

QED accounts for the whole life of a photon, from being emitted by an electron to being absorbed by another. This might sound small in scope, but pretty much every process in the Universe involves the exchange of photons and electrons. Moreover, scientists now know that atoms are bound together by a constant exchange of energy between the nucleus and electrons. This is actually an exchange of photons.

Feynman used diagrams like these to show how electrons and photons interact. The lines show their probable journey through time and space, like lines on a graph. The solid lines are electrons; the wavy lines are photons.

In QED, light is a particle. Its wave-like qualities come from the fact that we can only know its probable behaviour. **Refraction**, **reflection**, and every other effect involving light are not caused by waves. They are the accumulated effect of the probable behaviour of countless **quanta** or photons of light.

QED showed that reflection never involves photons bouncing off mirrors. Instead, the photons are absorbed by electrons of atoms in the glass and, an instant later, these electrons emit new photons. In that instant the electrons have moved around the atom a little, and so the new photons are emitted in a new direction. This is why we see the reflection at an angle.

Sometimes you see reflections in a window as well as the view outside. QED explains this very well.

THAT'S AMAZING!

Newton always puzzled over why, when you look out into the dark through a window at night, you see some of both the reflection of the room and the view outside. The thicker the glass is, the more you see of the reflection and the less you see outside.

The wave theory of light could always explain this by vaguely saying that light waves must "interfere" with each other in some way inside the glass. Yet it was hard to explain in terms of photons. The photons that form the reflection must bounce off the front surface of the glass like balls off a wall. Yet balls bounce the same off a wall, however thick the wall. So why would more photons bounce off thick glass than thin?

QED explains this very simply by revealing that no photons bounce off the front of the glass at all. Instead, the reflection is formed by photons that penetrate into the glass, then are absorbed and then are emitted by electrons in the glass. The thicker the glass, the more chance photons have of hitting an electron and being re-emitted towards your eyes as a reflection.

Playing with light

These diagrams show how a ruby laser works. An ordinary flash tube sets in motion a chain reaction of excited atoms, all emitting light at the same **wavelength**, in perfect step.

In the 1960s discoveries about light came together to create two new technologies that would transform our lives – **lasers** and **fibre optics**.

In 1917 Einstein had wondered if it was possible to stimulate a chain reaction in light. When a **photon** hits an **electron** in an **atom**, the electron is pushed to a higher energy level. Einstein thought that the atom might sometimes stay "primed" in this way, like a loaded gun. Then, when hit by another photon, it would not only emit a similar photon but also release another one. If the atom were surrounded by similarly primed atoms, this could start a chain reaction, releasing a flood of light.

In 1954 Russians Nikolai Basov (1922–2001) and Aleksandr Prokhorov (1916–2002) found that they could stimulate such a chain reaction in ammonia gas to generate microwaves. Americans Charles Townes (born 1915) and Arthur Schawlow (born 1921) wondered if they could achieve the same effect with visible light, and by 1960 Theodore Maiman (born 1927) succeeded.

The ruby laser

Maiman's giant device, which he called "laser", had a rod of ruby at its heart and gave a deep red light. Atoms in the ruby were primed or "excited" by a brief flash of light. The excited atoms then released photons, which zipped to and fro through the ruby as they were **reflected** off mirrors at either end.

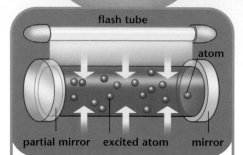

1. Light from the flash tube excites atoms in the ruby.

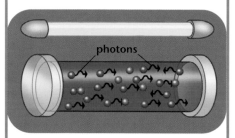

2. Excited atoms emit photons, which zip to and fro, bouncing off the mirrors at either end. As they go, the photons hit and excite more atoms.

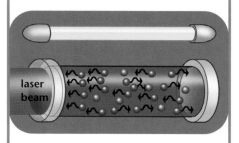

3. A flood of photons bursts through the partial mirror to create a beam of laser light.

Each time the photons went through the ruby they hit more excited atoms, releasing more photons. Eventually, the flood of photons was so intense that it flashed through the partially silvered mirror at one end, sending out a bright laser beam.

Laser light is unlike any other light. Other light is said to be "incoherent" because countless different photons are released spasmodically in all directions. With laser light, the photons are all identical and in sync. The result is an intense beam of light, of a single colour, which is much harder to scatter than ordinary light. In fact, laser light can be bounced off the Moon and back and still stays in a tight beam.

Lasers have developed greatly since Maiman's room-sized device. They have an incredible range of uses, from reading CDs to eye surgery.

THAT'S AMAZING!

The free-electron laser is a new type of laser being developed. It shoots tiny clouds of electrons at very high speeds between magnets. The magnets shake the electrons from side to side and make them release their energy in bursts of photons. Their light is 10 billion times more focused than laser light, and will allow scientists to photograph **DNA** in 3D and electrons jumping between atoms.

A laser light show is an impressive entertainment used at major events.

Fibre optics enable doctors to see inside the body. Fibre-optic cables are threaded into the body and transmit a picture from inside that can be seen on a screen. This helps doctors to identify internal problems and perform operations.

Fibre optics

The invention of the laser gave a dramatic boost to the barely developed technology of fibre optics. The origin of fibre optics dates back to 1854, when English scientist John Tyndall noticed how light seems to be trapped in a stream of water. Scientists in the 1950s found a way to use glass fibres to see inside the body. Lasers opened up the possibility of using these fibres for telecommunication.

Fibre-optic cables are made from bundles of glass-like fibres which transmit light by reflecting it off their internal surfaces. The light hits the surface of each fibre at such a shallow angle that it is reflected entirely inside the fibre.

Lasers made the perfect light for fibre optics. Words and pictures, speech, music, video, and many other kinds of data could be transformed into pulses of laser light and bounced down the fibre-optic cable at the speed of light. Fibre-optic cables can carry much more data much more quickly than conventional copper cables, which carry electrical signals. Optic cables can transmit data across the world in a fraction of a second.

Light speed communication

Since fibre-optic communication was introduced in the 1970s, it has transformed telecommunications. The first undersea optic cable, laid under the Atlantic in 1988, could carry more data than all the copper cables ever made in the world. Today, most big, long-distance connections are fibre optics.

Increasingly, fibre optics are linking right into homes, enabling things such as interactive TV on your computer. When this happens, there will be no need for satellite dishes and TV aerials; everything will come into your home by your Internet connection.

The glass fibres in a telephone cable are very thin, but they carry a huge amount of information, turned into light.

WHAT ARE PHOTONICS?

Electronic equipment, such as computers, depends on **semiconductor** devices such as silicon chips to control electricity. In the 1980s American scientist Eli Yablonovitch and others discovered that special photonic crystals can control light in the same way. Now scientists hope to swap silicon chips and electricity in computers for **photonic crystals** and beams of light, creating computers that run at the speed of light.

Since photons of light are tiny and almost without mass, these computers could be incredibly small and light. Many optical fibres are already being made with photonic crystals. They transmit signals even faster and more clearly than conventional fibres.

Changing light speed

Light is supposed to be the fastest thing in the Universe, always travelling at the same speed. In recent years some dramatic discoveries have reminded scientists that this is a simplification.

In the 1980s scientists used **lasers** to find the most accurate speed for light yet – 299,792,458 metres (186,282 miles) per second. Of course, to get a figure this accurate, they had to decide exactly what a second and a metre are. To give measurements that would never change, they used known waves of light. They defined the metre in terms of a certain number of **wavelengths** of light from a laser called a krypton-86. They defined a second as the time it takes for waves of light from caesium-133 **atoms** to vibrate a certain number of times.

Yet scientists realized that the only constant in the Universe is the speed of light. Time and distance vary with where you measure them – which means that neither the metre nor the second can be totally reliable. Therefore, in 1983, scientists decided to fix the speed of light forever at 299,792,458 metres (186,282 miles) per second. In future, if there are better measurements of the speed of light, it will be the metre that changes, not the speed.

THAT'S AMAZING!

The amazing thing about light in space is how long it goes on travelling in a straight line. We see stars because countless photons reach our eyes having travelled far across space. Photons from the furthest galaxies have been whizzing along in a straight line at almost 300,000 kilometres (186,000 miles) per second for over 12 billion years!

Has the speed changed?

Some scientists have questioned whether the speed of light is so constant. Could it have been faster in the earliest days of the Universe? If the Universe is 13.7 billion years old, as scientists estimate, then the furthest that light can ever have travelled is 13.7 billion light years. (A light year is the distance that light travels in a year.) The very furthest reaches of space are twice that distance apart – yet are so similar that they must all have been affected by the same light once. How could the same light affect them if they are twice as far apart as light could travel in the whole life of the Universe?

This telescope image, taken in 2004, shows the IR1916 galaxy (ringed). It is thought by some scientists to be 13.23 billion light years away. If so, it is the most distant object ever seen. The light we see has been travelling towards us since barely half a billion years after the Universe began.

The usual answer is that, in the earliest moments of the Universe, space itself expanded much faster than the speed of light, and so light didn't actually need to travel so far. In 1999 Portuguese-born physicist Doctor Joao Magueijo (born 1968) made a different suggestion – that the speed of light was much faster in the past. As yet, only a few scientists agree with this idea.

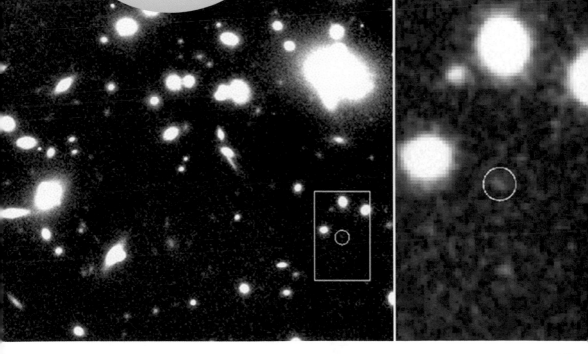

Freezing light

When scientists talk about the speed of light, they mean the speed of light in a vacuum. Light travels slightly more slowly in air, about 25 per cent more slowly in water, and more slowly still in diamonds. Nevertheless, these speeds are still so fast that the distance from Earth to the Sun could be travelled in a matter of minutes. Yet, in 1998, Danish scientist Lene Vestergaard Hau (born 1959) and her team at Rowland Institute in Cambridge, Massachusetts, slowed light down to the speed of an aeroplane. In 1999 they slowed it to the speed of a bicycle. In 2000 they stopped it altogether.

Hau succeeded by blasting two laser beams through a tiny cigar-shaped vessel. The vessel contained sodium atoms chilled to a few millionths of a degree above **absolute zero** (–273.15 °Celsius, or –459.67 °Fahrenheit). At this low temperature, the sodium atoms were in a very special state called a **Bose-Einstein Condensate** (BEC).

Normally there are assumed to be four states of matter – solid, liquid, gas, and **plasma**. Yet, back in the 1920s, Einstein and a young Indian scientist called Satyendra Bose (1894–1974) suggested that intense cold or pressure could create a special fifth state, the BEC.

Lene Vestergaard Hau is head of a team of scientists who have slowed down light to a complete stop.

Cold matter

Until the 1990s the Bose-Einstein Condensate was just theory. Then, in 1995, Eric Cornell (born 1961) and Carl Wiemann (born 1951) of Colorado University cooled rubidium gas to within a few millionths of a degree of absolute zero. This was the world's first known BEC. Soon scientists were making BECs regularly, with cooled rubidium or sodium atoms.

What is significant about a BEC is that all the atoms are in a very special state. Niels Bohr showed in 1913 that **electrons** can have different energy levels. So can atoms. At the very low temperatures of a BEC all atoms are, uniquely, in the same minimum-energy state. The result is that **photons** interact with them in slow motion. This is what slowed down and then stopped light in Hau's experiments.

This is a laboratory at the Massachusetts Institute of Technology, where research into Bose-Einstein Condensates is carried out.

THAT'S AMAZING!

It is impossible to study what happens to light when it is dragged into a **black hole** in space, because the power of the black hole's gravity stops light and any information escaping. Scientists Ulf Leonhardt and Paul Piwnicki suggest, however, that you could make mini black holes in the laboratory, using Bose-Einstein Condensates and slow light. In that way, scientists could study at their leisure the whirlpool of light spiralling slowly down into the hole.

Faster than light?

Einstein said that nothing moves faster than light. Yet in 2000 Chinese-born Ljun Wang (born 1957), of Princeton University in the USA, sent a laser pulse at 100 billion metres per second through a container of caesium gas. That's 310 times faster than light. Indeed, the pulses moved so fast that they seemed to have travelled back in time, emerging from the container before they entered.

In recent years scientists have often exceeded the light speed limit. Wang's was just the fastest. The scientists each have their own methods, but all involve "quantum tunnelling".

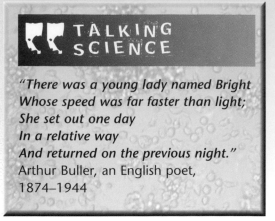

TALKING SCIENCE

"There was a young lady named Bright Whose speed was far faster than light; She set out one day In a relative way And returned on the previous night."
Arthur Buller, an English poet, 1874–1944

To understand this, imagine running into a brick wall. You expect to crash. However, quantum theory is about probability – and every now and then the improbable happens and you run straight through the wall. This never happens on a human scale, but it does on the level of **subatomic particles**. There are countless photons in a beam of light, and every now and then one jumps through a barrier that seems impenetrable. This is called tunnelling, but the photon does not actually burrow through – it jumps instantaneously to the far side. The effect is that it travels faster than light.

Speedy music

The subject of superluminary (faster-than-light) travel is controversial. Many scientists argue that these quantum jumps do not really break the light speed limit because no information is carried across.

Yet, in 1995, German scientist Günter Nimtz beamed Mozart's 40th symphony on a pulse of microwaves to a personal music player at 4.7 times the speed of light. This, he said, shows that information can travel faster than light. Other scientists argued that this is an illusion.

In the 1920s, Einstein predicted what would happen if one energetic photon split into two less energetic ones. According to quantum theory, Einstein said, the nature of the two new photons is not fixed until they are observed. Yet the instant that one is observed, the other's nature becomes fixed too – even if it is on the other side of the Universe.

Einstein thought this absurd, but scientists now know that the effect – called **quantum entanglement** – is real. The two photons are said to be "entangled" and can be used as a **teleporter**. You attach things (such as another photon) to one, and instantly the attachment is recreated by the other. In 1997 photons were teleported in this way across a lab in Rome. Scientists talk of one day teleporting objects instantly across the world like this – but it is a long way off!

A teleportation experiment is carried out at the University of Innsbruck, Austria, in June 2004.

Future light

Our understanding of light has come a long way in the last few hundred years. Gradually the **quantum** idea that light is particles has replaced the idea that light is waves, which once seemed so certain. Waves remain the simplest way to explain some of the behaviour of light, such as **refraction**, and some scientists still talk of a wave-particle duality. However, most accept that the wave is just a way of describing the combined movement of countless **photons**.

Until the last century, people relied mostly on natural light from the Sun, and nights were generally dark. Now, our cities are filled day and night with a dazzling display of artificial light, and few places on the surface of Earth are ever utterly dark.

In 2006, scientists at Imperial College, London, announced that they had found a way to make an invisibility cloak, like fictional wizard Harry Potter's! The idea is to make the cloak or shield with man-made "meta" materials, which allow light rays to flow around them as water flows around a stone. The rays meet up again on the far side undisturbed. The scientists hope first to create a cloak that is invisible to microwaves, then one that is invisible to light.

We know that the life of a light particle, or photon, is in essence quite simple. Photons are emitted from excited **electrons** of **atoms**. Then they travel at high speed in straight lines until they encounter other electrons, which absorb them. New photons may then be emitted from the electrons.

Alongside this deceptively simple picture, some astonishing discoveries have been made. These have already overturned our understanding of the Universe and led to technology that has revolutionized our lives. Scientists now experiment with ways to control light so completely that they can slow it to a stop, or send things across space much faster than the speed of light. There is every possibility that the future could be filled with even more amazing revelations and technologies.

THAT'S AMAZING!

Science-fiction writers are talking about "slow glass". This could be a window through which light travels so slowly that you could pack it up, take it round the world, and then see the view outside months later. They are also talking about crystal memories – little cubic crystals no bigger than a dice, criss-crossed with flashes of light embedded by **laser** beams. These could hold the memory of every book in the world, or the entire Internet. Who knows what the future will bring?

Timeline

BC

c.400 Mo-Tzu notes that light travels in straight lines and that pinholes can create images in dark rooms.

c.300 Euclid notices that light rays are reflected at the same angle as they strike a surface.

c.200 Diocles notices how a curved reflecting surface can focus light rays.

AD

140 Ptolemy notes that refraction varies according to the angle at which light strikes a surface.

c.1000 Alhazen realizes that light is emitted by hot light sources.

c.1000 Ibn Sahl invents the lens.

c.1267 Roger Bacon has the idea that combining two lenses might make a device for magnifying things.

1608 Hans Lippershey makes an eyeglass with two lenses for magnifying distant things.

1609 Galileo makes the first high-powered telescope.

1665 Robert Hooke is one of the first to use a microscope.

1666 Isaac Newton realizes that white light can be split into all colours with a prism.

c.1670 Newton invents the reflecting telescope.

c.1670 Newton suggests that light rays consist of tiny particles.

1675 Ole Römer works out that light takes several minutes to reach Earth from Jupiter. Christiaan Huygens uses Römer's figures to work out the speed of light.

1678 Huygens suggests that light travels in waves.

1728 James Bradley works out the speed of light more accurately using starlight.

1800 William Herschel discovers infrared light.

1801 Johann Ritter discovers ultraviolet light.

1801 Thomas Young's double-slit experiment provides evidence for the wave theory of light.

1808 Thomas Young and Augustin Fresnel develop the idea of the polarization of light.

1826 Joseph Niépce makes the world's first photograph.

1837 Jacques Louis Daguerre develops the first successful photographic process.

1846 Michael Faraday announces his theory that light is a wave related to electricity and magnetism.

1850 Jean Foucault makes the first accurate measurement of the speed of light.

1854 John Tyndall observes the phenomenon of total internal reflection.

1860 Robert Bunsen and Gustav Kirchhoff discover emission and absorption spectra.

1865 James Clerk Maxwell shows that light is a form of electromagnetic radiation.

1868 Norman Lockyer and Pierre Janssen each predict the existence of a new element, helium, by analysing the spectrum of sunlight.

1878 William Crookes invents the cathode ray tube.

1885 Johann Balmer discovers a mathematical relationship between the colours in the spectrum of hydrogen.

1887 Albert Michelson and Edward Morley show that the speed of light is the same in all directions.

1888 Heinrich Hertz discovers radio waves.

1898 Wilhelm Röntgen discovers X-rays.

1900 Max Planck introduces the idea of quanta to explain how light is emitted by a glowing surface.

1902 Philipp Lenard explores the photoelectric effect.

1905 Albert Einstein explains the photoelectric effect by reviving the idea that light travels in particles, later called photons.

1906 Einstein publishes his Theory of Special Relativity, showing that the speed of light never varies.

1912 Niels Bohr develops his theory of the atom and how it emits light in terms of energy levels.

1916 Einstein proposes the idea of stimulated emission of light.

1923 Arthur Compton proves that photons exist.

1924 Louis de Broglie shows that electrons can be waves.

1927 Werner Heisenberg develops the uncertainty principle.

1928 Bohr suggests that light can be a wave and a particle.

1950 Richard Feynman and others develop the theory of quantum electrodynamics.

1958 Arthur Schawlow and Charles Townes develop the theory of the laser.

1960 Theodore Maiman builds the first laser.

c.1985 Eli Yablonovitch discovers photonic crystals.

c.1997 Particles are teleported across a lab by quantum entanglement.

1999 Joao Magueijo suggests that the speed of light may have been different in the past.

2000 Lene Vestergaard Hau and her team stop a light beam.

2000 Ljun Wang sends a beam of light at 310 times faster than the speed of light.

2006 Scientists suggest a way to make an invisibility cloak.

Biographies

These are some of the leading scientists in the story of light.

Isaac Newton (1642–1727)

Born in the village of Woolsthorpe in Lincolnshire, Isaac Newton was the greatest English scientist of all time. His discoveries began when he was a student at Cambridge and showed that all the colours of light are contained in "white" daylight. Later he came up with the idea that light in rays moves as tiny particles or "corpuscles". In 1665, an outbreak of plague made him return to Woolsthorpe, and it was there that he laid the foundations of his theory of gravity and his three laws of motion, which underpin all modern physics. He also invented the reflecting telescope. He returned to Cambridge as a professor in 1669, and stayed there until 1687, when he went to London as a Member of Parliament. In 1696, Newton became Master of the Royal Mint, a post he kept until he died.

Christiaan Huygens (1629–1693)

Born in The Hague in Holland, Huygens was the brightest star of the Golden Age of Dutch science, but he spent most of his adult life in Paris. Like many scientists of his day, he had wide-ranging interests. He made many discoveries with microscopes and telescopes that he made himself. His telescopes were so good that he was able to discover Saturn's moon Titan and the nature of Saturn's rings. He also mapped the surface of Mars and identified stars in the tiny blotch of light in the night sky known as the Orion nebula. He is most famous for inventing the pendulum clock and for his wave theory of light, which gave a much better explanation of reflection and refraction than Newton's rival particle theory.

Thomas Young (1773–1829)

Thomas Young was the youngest of 10 children in a Quaker family from Milverton in Somerset, England. By the age of 14 he had learned 12 languages: Greek, Latin, French, Italian, Hebrew, Chaldean, Syriac, Samaritan, Arabic, Persian, Turkish, and Amharic. At university, he studied medicine and then physics. In science he is most famous for his double-slit experiment, which was strong evidence for the wave theory of light, and for his theory, now proven, that our eyes respond only to three basic colours.

James Clerk Maxwell (1831–1879)

Born in Edinburgh in Scotland, James Clerk Maxwell was so reserved and slow as a child that he was nicknamed "Dafty". Then, at the age of 14, he surprised everyone with a brilliant essay about how to draw mathematical curves with a piece of string. From then on, Maxwell quickly became perhaps the greatest scientist and mathematician of the 19th century. While professor of natural philosophy at King's College, London, he developed the idea of electromagnetic fields, and showed that light is just one form of electromagnetic radiation. In a brilliant proof that we see all colours as mixes of just three basic ones, he made the world's first colour photograph in 1861. He also made contributions to the molecular theory of gases and to the science of astrophysics.

Albert Einstein (1879–1955)

Born in Ulm in Germany, Einstein did not show his genius at first. He was rejected by several universities and went to work at the patent office in Bern, Switzerland, in 1902. However, within three years he had written five papers, each of which would make a profound impact on science. In the first, explaining how light could create electricity, he showed that light could be particles (later called photons), not waves. Another paper helped prove the existence of atoms. The most important was his Theory of Special Relativity, where he explained that only the speed of light is constant – every other movement is relative – and explored the implications of this. Nuclear power and nuclear weapons stem from the way Einstein linked energy and mass in this theory. By 1915, he had developed his General Theory of Relativity, giving a revolutionary new explanation of gravity. By the time Einstein moved to the United States in 1933, he was the most famous scientist in the world.

Niels Bohr (1885–1962)

Born in Copenhagen in Denmark, Bohr came from a high-achieving family, his father being a professor of physiology and his brother an international soccer star, as well as a mathematician. Niels was also a talented soccer player. After receiving a PhD from Copenhagen University in 1911, he worked in England with Ernest Rutherford, who was making discoveries about the nature of the atom. This led Bohr to develop his own theory, explaining how light is emitted from atoms in terms of energy levels. Bohr then played a key part in developing the wave-particle duality – the theory that light can be both a wave and a particle. In the Second World War he fled to the United States and worked on the project to develop the atomic bomb. Later he championed the peaceful use of nuclear energy.

Richard Feynman (1918–1988)

Born in Far Rockaway in New York City, Feynman (said "FINE-man") was the son of Jewish parents. One of the main American scientists of the 20th century, he won the Nobel Prize for Physics in 1965 for his part in developing the quantum electrodynamic (QED) theory of light and subatomic particles. He also contributed to the idea of subatomic particles called quarks, and to the science of supercooled liquids. He helped in the development of the atomic bomb and headed the panel that investigated the Space Shuttle *Challenger* disaster of 1986.

Glossary

absolute zero lowest temperature possible, at which even atoms stop moving. It is equivalent to −273.15 °Celsius or −459.67 °Fahrenheit.

after-image picture that persists in the eye after the stimulus that created it has gone

atom smallest possible part of an element

black hole object in space that has collapsed under its own gravity. Its gravitational pull then intensifies so much that even light cannot escape.

Bose-Einstein Condensate special state of matter, first suggested by Einstein and Bose, which occurs at very cold temperatures near absolute zero. Atoms all have the minimum possible energy, and so begin to act as one.

camera obscura special darkened room with a small hole or lens which lets in light to project an image of the outside world

cathode rays streams of electrons emitted from the negative terminal in a vacuum tube

chemical element substance that cannot be broken down into simpler substances

chromatic aberration blurring in a telescope or camera caused by colours refracting differently through the lens

corpuscles Newton's name for particles of light

diffraction spreading or bending of light as it passes through a small hole or around the edge of an object in its path

DNA chemical that carries in its structure the basic instructions for life in all living things

electromagnetic radiation energy, such as light and radio waves, that is emitted from atoms in the form of waves of electricity and magnetism

electrons principal particles of an atom outside the nucleus. Each electron has a negative electrical charge.

fibre optics technology of sending light through flexible glass fibres

gamma rays electromagnetic radiation emitted by excited atomic nuclei

geometry mathematics of space and angles

helium very light, colourless gas. Only hydrogen is lighter and more common in the Universe.

Iceland spar special clear crystals of the mineral calcite, which give a double image when you look through them

image picture created by a lens or mirror or just a pinhole

interference interaction between two or more waves

laser special, very intense, pure form of light. Uniquely, the waves are all equal in length and perfectly in step. *Laser* stands for *l*ight *a*mplification by *s*timulated *e*mission of *r*adiation.

momentum tendency of a moving object to stay moving in the same direction at the same speed due to its mass

nucleus core of an atom

optical relating to light and lenses

photoelectric effect release of electrons from substances exposed to light

photonic crystals crystals that change the degree to which they transmit light according to the way that they are stimulated by light

photons basic particles of light

plasma fourth state of matter, after solid, liquid, and gas, in which gas particles are electrically charged

polarized light light in which waves vibrate only in one plane

primary colours three basic colours that can be mixed to make all other colours

prism triangular wedge of glass

probability likelihood of something happening

quantum minimum amount by which something such as energy can change

quantum electrodynamics (QED) study of electromagnetism in quantum terms

quantum entanglement quantum effect by which two particles can behave as one, even if they are very far apart

reflection how light is bounced back from a surface

refraction how light rays may be bent as they pass from one transparent substance to another

semiconductor substance that can be changed to either conduct or block electricity

spectrum continuous array of different things, such as the rainbow spread of colours created by passing light through a prism, or the entire range of electromagnetic radiation

subatomic particles particles smaller than an atom

teleporter device for sending an object through space instantly

uncertainty principle Heisenberg's theory that you can be sure about a particle's position or its momentum – but never both at the same time

wavelength distance between one peak of a wave and the next, or between one trough and the next

Further resources

If you have enjoyed this book and want to find out more, you can look at the following books and websites.

Books

DK Eyewitness Science: Light
David Burnie
(Dorling Kindersley, 1991)

How Science Works
Judith Hann
(Dorling Kindersley, 1991)

Light Action!
Vicki Cobb
(HarperCollins,1993)

Light up Your Life
D. Phillips
(Portland Press, 1997)

The Story of Science: Newton at the Centre
Joy Hakim
(Smithsonian Books, 2005)

Websites

www.opticsforkids.com/optics _for_kids.html
Optics for Kids
Entertaining site about light and the science of optics, with colourful graphics and plenty of fun experiments to carry out.

www.kidsclick.com/descrip/ zap.htm
Thinkin' Science: ZAP! Blaze
Although not free, this educational software is a great way to learn about lasers in a project in which you help a rock band fix the light show for their big concert.

http://micro.magnet.fsu. edu/primer/lightandcolor/ index.html
Molecular Expressions: Physics of Light and Color
Although a little more advanced, this site has a very clear rundown of all the basic concepts in light and colour, from the speed of light to the wave-particle duality.

http://acept.la.asu.edu/PiN/ mod/light/pattLightOptics. html
Patterns in Nature: Light and Optics
Arizona State University's site is a good basic introduction to light and optics.

www.exploratorium.edu/ snacks/iconlight.html
Snacks about Light
The San Francisco Exploratorium's "Snacks" site has some great activities about light for you to try.

Index

Titles in the *Chain Reactions* series include:

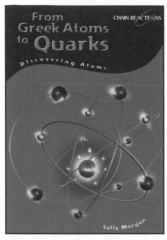

Hardback 978 0 431 18657 3

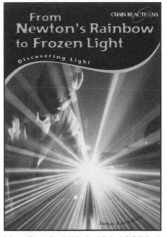

Hardback 978 0 431 18658 0

Hardback 978 0 431 18659 7

Hardback 978 0 431 18660 3

Hardback 978 0 431 18661 0

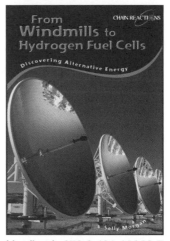

Hardback 978 0 431 18662 7

Find out about other titles from Heinemann Library on our website www.heinemann.co.uk/library